My Favorite Animal

I LOVE LIZARDS!

By Beth Gottlieb

Gareth Stevens
PUBLISHING

Please visit our website, www.garethstevens.com. For a free color catalog of all our high-quality books, call toll free 1-800-542-2595 or fax 1-877-542-2596.

Library of Congress Cataloging-in-Publication Data
Names: Gottlieb, Beth, author.
Title: I love lizards! / Beth Gottlieb.
Description: Buffalo, New York : Gareth Stevens Publishing, [2023] | Series: My favorite animal | Includes index.
Identifiers: LCCN 2022014031 (print) | LCCN 2022014032 (ebook) | ISBN 9781538283271 (paperback) | ISBN 9781538283295 (library binding) | ISBN 9781538283301 (ebook)
Subjects: LCSH: Lizards–Juvenile literature.
Classification: LCC QL666.L2 G68 2023 (print) | LCC QL666.L2 (ebook) | DDC 597.95–dc23/eng/20220520
LC record available at https://lccn.loc.gov/2022014031
LC ebook record available at https://lccn.loc.gov/2022014032

First Edition

Published in 2023 by
Gareth Stevens Publishing
2544 Clinton St,
Buffalo, NY 14224

Editor: Kristen Nelson
Designer: Rachel Rising

Photo credits: Cover, p. 1 John Slawik/Shutterstock.com; p. 5 Elena Sherengovskaya/Shutterstock.com; p. 7 Christian_Schmidt/Shutterstock.com; p. 7 Mufti Adi Utomo/Shutterstock.com; p. 7 Jillian Cain Photography/ Shutterstock.com; p. 7 Elana Yakubov/Shutterstock.com; pp. 9, 24 Chaikom/Shutterstock.com; pp. 11, 24 Carrie Beth Hamilton/Shutterstock.com; pp. 13, 24 J.NATAYO/Shutterstock.com; p. 15 Ewa Studio/Shutterstock.com; p. 17 BLFootage/Shutterstock.com; p. 19 Dudley Simpson/Shutterstock.com; p. 21 Chuck Wagner/Shutterstock.com; p. 23 Michael Shake/Shutterstock.com.

Printed in the United States of America

CPSIA compliance information: Batch #CWGS23: For further information contact Gareth Stevens, New York, New York at 1-800-542-2595.

Find us on

Contents

Cool Lizards 4

Lizard Bodies 8

Families 12

What Color? 18

Words to Know 24

Index. 24

I love lizards!

There are many kinds.
They live all over
the world.

They have scales.

Most lose their skin as they grow.
This is molting.

Most lay eggs.
The eggs are soft.

Babies look like
their parents.

Lizards can be big
or small.
Geckos are small.

They can be
many colors.
Many are green
or brown.

Iguanas are green
or blue.
Males turn orange
or red!

You can see them at the zoo!

Words to Know

eggs

molting

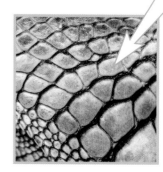
scales

Index

babies, 14

eggs, 12

color, 18, 20

size, 16